The Gospel of the Nativity of Mary

By St. Matthew

Copyright © 2020 Lamp of Trismegistus. All rights reserved. No part of this publication may be reproduced or transmitted in any form or by any means, electronic or mechanical, including photocopying, recording, or by any information storage and retrieval system, without permission in writing from Lamp of Trismegistus. Reviewers may quote brief passages.

ISBN: 978-1-63118-448-2

Christian Apocrypha Series

Other Books in this Series and Related Titles

The Testament of Abraham by Abraham (978-1-63118-441-3)

Psalms of Solomon by King Solomon (978-1-63118-439-0)

The Lives of Adam and Eve by Moses (978-1-63118-414-7)

The Testament of Moses by Moses (978-1-63118-440-6)

The Secrets of Enoch by Enoch (978-1-63118-449-9)

The First and Second Gospels of the Infancy of Jesus Christ by Thomas and James (978-1-63118-415-4)

Lost Chapters of the Book of Daniel and Related Writings by Daniel (978-1-63118-417-8)

The Book of the Watchers by Enoch (978-1-63118-416-1)

The Book of Parables by Enoch (978-1-63118-429-1)

Book of Dreams by Enoch (978-1-63118-437-6)

The Book of Astronomical Secrets by Enoch (978-1-63118-443-7)

Masonic Symbolism of Easter and the Christ in Masonry by various authors (978-1-63118-434-5)

A Few Masonic Sermons by A. C. Ward & Bascom B. Clarke (978-1-63118-435-2)

Masonic Symbolism of King Solomon's Temple by Albert G. Mackey & others (978-1-63118-442-0)

Audio Versions are also Available on Audible and iTunes

Table of Contents

Introduction...7

Prologue...9

Part I
Translation by Archbishop of Canterbury William Wake
Chapter I...11
Chapter II...13
Chapter III...17
Chapter IV...19
Chapter V...21
Chapter VI...25
Chapter VII...27
Chapter VIII...31

Part II
Translation by James Donaldson & Alexander Roberts
Chapter I...33
Chapter II...35
Chapter III...37
Chapter IV...39
Chapter V...41
Chapter VI...43
Chapter VII...45
Chapter VIII...47
Chapter IX...49
Chapter X...51

Introduction

The Apocrypha are a loosely knit series of books, written by early vanguards of Christianity (covering the eras of both the old and new testaments), and which comprise somewhere between about a dozen to several hundred titles, depending on whom you ask and how that person defines "Apocrypha." A small selection of these can still be found included in the Catholic bible, while a majority of the books in question, were abandoned by church officials in the early centuries of Christianity. Many of these apocryphal books were originally considered canon by early followers of Christ, in the first four centuries following his birth. It wasn't until the meeting of the Council of Nicaea in 325, that Emperor Constantine and a group of roughly 300 church bishops, gathered together with the goal of defining, standardizing and unifying an otherwise splintering Christianity, that many of these writings ceased to be included in the newly established canon. Enjoy then, this book as an example, of just one of the many books of the Christian Apocrypha, and be sure to check out other titles in this series.

Prologue

Here we are presenting two different translations of the *Gospel of the Birth of Mary*, also known as the *Gospel of the Nativity of Mary*, which was originally attributed to Saint Matthew. The first was translated in the early eighteenth century by the Archbishop of Canterbury, William Wake. The second translation dates to the late nineteenth century and was a collaboration between James Donaldson and Alexander Roberts. The pair worked together translating 24 volumes of early Christian texts from Greek and Latin, into English. It should be noted that even though the two translations have a different number of chapters, the first having 8, the second having 10, the two translations cover the same material.

PART I

The Gospel of the Nativity of Mary

Translated by William Wake

CHAPTER I

The blessed and ever glorious Virgin Mary, sprung from the royal race and family of David, was born in the city of Nazareth, and educated at Jerusalem, in the temple of the Lord.

Her father's name was Joachim, and her mother's Anna. The family of her father was of Galilee and the city of Nazareth. The family of her mother was of Bethlehem.

Their lives were plain and right in the sight of the Lord, pious and faultless before men. For they divided all their substance into three parts:

One of which they devoted to the temple and officers of the temple; another they distributed among strangers, and persons in poor circumstances; and the third they reserved for themselves and the uses of their own family.

In this manner they lived for about twenty years chastely, in the favor of God, and the esteem of men, without any children.

But they vowed, if God should favor them with any issue, they would devote it to the service of the Lord; on which account they went at every feast in the year to the temple of the Lord

And it came to pass, that when the feast of the dedication drew near, Joachim, with some others of his tribe, went up to Jerusalem, and at that time, Issachar was high-priest;

Who, when he saw Joachim along with the rest of his neighbors, bringing his offering, despised both him and his offerings, and asked him,

Why he, who had no children, would presume to appear among those who had? Adding, that his offerings could never be acceptable to God, who was judged by him unworthy to have children; the Scripture having said, Cursed is every one who shall not beget a male in Israel.

He further said, that he ought first to be free from that curse by begetting some issue, and then come with his offerings into the presence of God.

But Joachim being much confounded with the shame of such reproach, retired to the shepherds, who were with the cattle in their pastures;

For he was not inclined to return home, lest his neighbors, who were present and heard all this from the high-priest, should publicly reproach him in the same manner.

CHAPTER II

But when he had been there for some time, on a certain day when he was alone, the angel of the Lord stood by him with a prodigious light.

To whom, being troubled at the appearance, the angel who had appeared to him, endeavoring to compose him said:

Be not afraid, Joachim, nor troubled at the sight of me, for I am an angel of the Lord sent by him to you, that I might inform you, that your prayers are heard, and your alms ascended in the sight of God.

For he hath surely seen your shame, and heard you unjustly reproached for not having children: for God is the avenger of sin, and not of nature;

And so when he shuts the womb of any person, he does it for this reason, that he may in a more wonderful manner again open it, and that which is born appear to be not the product of lust, but the gift of God.

For the first mother of your nation Sarah, was she not barren even till her eightieth year: And yet even in the end of her old age brought forth Isaac, in whom the promise was made a blessing to all nations.

Rachel also, so much in favor with God, and beloved so much by holy Jacob, continued barren for a long time, yet afterwards was the mother of Joseph, who was not only governor of Egypt, but delivered many nations from perishing with hunger.

Who among the judges was more valiant than Samson, or more holy than Samuel? And yet both their mothers were barren.

But if reason will not convince you of the truth of my words, that there are frequent conceptions in advanced years, and that those who were barren have brought forth to their great surprise; therefore Anna your wife shall bring you a daughter, and you shall call her name Mary;

She shall, according to your vow, be devoted to the Lord from her infancy, and be filled with the Holy Ghost from her mother's womb;

She shall neither eat nor drink anything which is unclean, nor shall her conversation be without among the common people, but in the temple of the Lord; that so she may not fall under any slander or suspicion of what is bad.

So in the process of her years, as she shall be in a miraculous manner born of one that was barren, so she shall, while yet a virgin, in a way unparalleled, bring forth the Son of the most High God, who shall, be called Jesus, and, according to the signification of his name, be the Savior of all nations.

And this shall be a sign to you of the things which I declare, namely, when you come to the golden gate of Jerusalem, you shall there meet your wife Anna, who being very much troubled that you returned no sooner, shall then rejoice to see you.

When the angel had said this he departed from him.

CHAPTER III

Afterwards the angel appeared to Anna his wife saying: Fear not, neither think that which you see is a spirit.

For I am that angel who hath offered up your prayers and alms before God, and am now sent to you, that I may inform you, that a daughter will be born unto you, who shall be called Mary, and shall be blessed above all women.

She shall be, immediately upon her birth, full of the grace of the Lord, and shall continue during the three years of her weaning in her father's house, and afterwards, being devoted to the service of the Lord, shall not depart from the temple, till she arrives to years of discretion.

In a word, she shall there serve the Lord night and day in fasting and prayer, shall abstain from every unclean thing, and never know any man;

But, being an unparalleled instance without any pollution or defilement, and a virgin not knowing any man, shall bring forth a son, and a maid shall bring forth the Lord, who both by his grace and name and works, shall be the Savior of the world.

Arise therefore, and go up to Jerusalem, and when you shall come to that which is called the golden gate (because it is gilt with gold), as a sign of what I have told you, you shall meet your husband, for whose safety you have been so much concerned.

When therefore you find these things thus accomplished, believe that all the rest which I have told you, shall also undoubtedly be accomplished.

According therefore to the command of the angel, both of them left the places where they were, and when they came to the place specified in the angel's prediction, they met each other.

Then, rejoicing at each other's vision, and being fully satisfied in the promise of a child, they gave due thanks to the Lord, who exalts the humble.

After having praised the Lord, they returned home, and lived in a cheerful and assured expectation of the promise of God.

So Anna conceived, and brought forth a daughter, and, according to the angel's command, the parents did call her name Mary.

CHAPTER IV

And when three years were expired, and the time of her weaning complete, they brought the Virgin to the temple of the Lord with offerings.

And there were about the temple, according to the fifteen Psalms of degrees, fifteen stairs to ascend.

For the temple being built in a mountain, the altar of burnt-offering, which was without, could not be come near but by stairs;

The parents of the blessed Virgin and infant Mary put her upon one of these stairs;

But while they were putting off their clothes, in which they had travelled, and according to custom putting on some that were more neat and clean,

In the meantime the Virgin of the Lord in such a manner went up all the stairs one after another, without the help of any to lead or lift her, that anyone would have judged from hence that she was of perfect age.

Thus the Lord did, in the infancy of his Virgin, work this extraordinary work, and evidence by this miracle how great she was like to be hereafter.

But the parents having offered up their sacrifice, according to the custom of the law, and perfected their vow, left the Virgin with other virgins in the apartments of the temple, who were to be brought up there, and they returned home.

CHAPTER V

But the Virgin of the Lord, as she advanced in fears, increased also in perfections, and according to the saying of the Psalmist, her father and mother forsook her, but the Lord took care of her.

For she every day had the conversation of angels, and every day received visitors from God, which preserved her from all sorts of evil, and caused her to abound with all good things;

So that when at length she arrived to her fourteenth year, as the wicked could not lay anything to her charge worthy of reproof, so all good persons, who were acquainted with her, admired her life and conversation.

At that time the high-priest made a public order. That all the virgins who had public settlements in the temple, and were come to this age, should return home, and, as they were now of a proper maturity, should, according to the custom of their country, endeavor to be married.

To which command, though all the other virgins readily yielded obedience, Mary the Virgin of the Lord alone answered, that she could not comply with it.

Assigning these reasons, that both she and her parents had devoted her to the service of the Lord; and besides, that she had vowed virginity to the Lord, which vow she was resolved never to break through by lying with a man.

The high priest being hereby brought into a difficulty,

Seeing he durst neither on the one hand dissolve the vow, and disobey the Scripture, which says, Vow and pay,

Nor on the other hand introduce a custom, to which the people were strangers, commanded,

That at the approaching feast all the principal persons both of Jerusalem and the neighboring places should meet together, that he might have their advice, how he had best proceed in so difficult a case.

When they were accordingly met, they unanimously agreed to seek the Lord, and ask counsel from him on this matter.

And when they were all engaged in prayer, the high-priest, according to the usual way, went to consult God.

And immediately there was a voice from the ark, and the mercy seat, which all present heard, that it must be inquired or sought out by a prophecy of Isaiah to whom the Virgin should be given and be betrothed;

For Isaiah saith, there shall come forth a rod out of the stem of Jesse, and a flower shall spring out of its root,

And the Spirit of the Lord shall rest upon him, the Spirit of Wisdom and Understanding, the Spirit of Counsel and Might, the Spirit of Knowledge and Piety, and the Spirit of the fear of the Lord shall fill him.

Then, according to this prophecy, he appointed, that all the men of the house and family of David, who were marriageable, and not married, should bring their several rods to the altar,

And out of whatsoever person's rod after it was brought, a flower should bud forth, and on the top of it the Spirit of the Lord should sit in the appearance of a dove, he should be the man to whom the Virgin should be given and be betrothed.

CHAPTER VI

Among the rest there was a man named Joseph, of the house and family of David, and a person very far advanced in years, who drew back his rod, when everyone besides presented his.

So that when nothing appeared agreeable to the heavenly voice, the high-priest judged it proper to consult God again,

Who answered that he to whom the Virgin was to be betrothed was the only person of those who were brought together, who had not brought his rod.

Joseph therefore was betrayed.

For, when he did bring his rod, and a dove coming from Heaven pitched upon the top of it, every one plainly saw, that the Virgin was to be betrothed to him:

Accordingly, the usual ceremonies of betrothing being over, he returned to his own city of Bethlehem, to set his house in order, and make the needful for the marriage.

But the Virgin of the Lord, Mary, with seven other virgins of the same age, who had been weaned at the same time, and who had been appointed to attend her by the priest, returned to her parents' house in Galilee.

CHAPTER VII

Now at this time of her first coming into Galilee, the angel Gabriel was sent to her from God, to declare to her the conception of our Savior, and the manner and way of her conceiving him.

Accordingly going into her, he filled the chamber where she was with a prodigious light, and in a most courteous manner saluting her, he said,

Hail, Mary! Virgin of the Lord most acceptable! O Virgin full of Grace! The Lord is with you, you are blessed above all women, you are blessed above all men, that. have been hitherto born.

But the Virgin, who had before been well acquainted with the countenances of angels, and to whom such light from heaven was no uncommon thing,

Was neither terrified with the vision of the angel, nor astonished at the greatness of the light, but only troubled about the angel's words:

And began to consider what so extraordinary a salutation should mean, what it did portend, or what sort of end it would have.

To this thought the angel, divinely inspired, replies;

Fear not, Mary, as though I intended anything inconsistent with your chastity in this salutation:

For you have found favor with the Lord, because you made virginity your choice.

Therefore while you are a Virgin, you shall conceive without sin, and bring forth a son.

He shall be great, because he shall reign from sea to sea, and from the rivers to the ends of the earth.

And he shall be called the Son of the Highest; for he who is born in a mean state on earth reigns in an exalted one in heaven.

And the Lord shall give him the throne of his father David, and he shall reign over the house of Jacob forever, and of his kingdom there shall be no end.

For he is the King of Kings, and Lord of Lords, and his throne is forever and ever.

To this discourse of the angel the Virgin replied not, as though she were unbelieving, but willing to know the manner of it.

She said, How can that be? For seeing, according to my vow, I have never known any man, how can I bear a child without the addition of a man's seed?

To this the angel replied and said, Think not, Mary, that you shall conceive in the ordinary way.

For, without lying with a man, while a Virgin, you shall conceive; while a Virgin, you shall bring forth; and while a Virgin shall give suck.

For the Holy Ghost shall come upon you, and the power of the Most High shall overshadow you, without any of the heats of lust.

So that which shall be born of you shall be only holy, because it only is conceived without sin, and being born, shall be called the Son of God.

Then Mary stretching forth her hands, and lifting her eyes to heaven, said, Behold the handmaid of the Lord! Let it be unto me according to thy word.

CHAPTER VIII

Joseph therefore went from Judaea to Galilee, with intention to marry the Virgin who was betrothed to him:

For it was now near three months since she was betrothed to him.

At length it plainly appeared she was with child, and it could not be hid from Joseph:

For going to the Virgin in a free manner, as one espoused, and talking familiarly with her, he perceived her to be with child.

And thereupon began to be uneasy and doubtful, not knowing what course it would be best to take;

For being a just man, he was not willing to expose her, nor defame her by the suspicion of being a whore, since he was a pious man.

He purposed therefore privately to put an end to their agreement, and as privately to put her away.

But while he was meditating these things, behold the angel of the Lord appeared to him in his sleep, and said Joseph, son of David, fear not;

Be not willing to entertain any suspicion of the Virgin's being guilty of fornication, or to think anything amiss of her, neither be afraid to take her to wife;

For that which is begotten In her and now distresses your mind, is not the work of man, but the Holy Ghost.

For she of all women is that only Virgin who shall bring forth the Son of God, and you shall call his name Jesus, that is, Savior: for he will save his people from their sins.

Joseph thereupon, according to the command of the angel, married the Virgin, and did not know her, but kept her in chastity.

And now the ninth month from her conception drew near, when Joseph took his wife and what other things were necessary to Bethlehem, the city from whence he came.

And it came to pass, while they were there, the days were fulfilled for her bringing forth.

And she brought forth her first-born son, as the holy Evangelists have taught, even our Lord Jesus Christ, who with the Father, Son, and Holy Ghost, lives and reigns to everlasting ages.

PART II

The Gospel of the Nativity of Mary

Translated by Donaldson and Roberts

CHAPTER I

The blessed and glorious ever-virgin Mary, sprung from the royal stock and family of David, born in the city of Nazareth, was brought up at Jerusalem in the temple of the Lord. Her father was named Joachim, and her mother Anna. Her father's house was from Galilee and the city of Nazareth, but her mother's family from Bethlehem. Their life was guileless and right before the Lord, and irreproachable and pious before men. For they divided all their substance into three parts. One part they spent upon the temple and the temple servants; another they distributed to strangers and the poor; the third they reserved, for themselves and the necessities of their family. Thus, dear to God, kind to men, for about twenty years they lived in their own house, a chaste married life, without having any children. Nevertheless they vowed that, should the Lord happen to give them offspring, they would deliver it to the service of the Lord; on which account also they used to visit the temple of the Lord at each of the feasts during the year.

CHAPTER II

And it came to pass that the festival of the dedication was at hand; wherefore also Joachim went up to Jerusalem with some men of his own tribe. Now at that time Issachar was high priest there. And when he saw Joachim with his offering among his other fellow-citizens, he despised him, and spurned his gifts, asking why he, who had no offspring, presumed to stand among those who had; saying that his gifts could not by any means be acceptable to God, since He had deemed him unworthy of off-spring: for the Scripture said, Cursed is every one who has not begot a male or a female in Israel. He said, therefore, that he ought first to be freed from this curse by the begetting of children; and then, and then only, that he should come into the presence of the Lord with his offerings. And Joachim, covered with shame from this reproach that was thrown in his teeth, retired to the shepherds, who were in their pastures with their flocks; nor would he return home, lest perchance he might be branded with the same reproach by those of his own tribe, who were there at the time, and had heard this from the priest.

CHAPTER III

Now, when he had been there for some time, on a certain day when he was alone, an angel of the Lord stood by him in a great light. And when he was disturbed at his appearance, the angel who had appeared to him restrained his fear, saying: Fear not, Joachim, nor be disturbed by my appearance; for I am the angel of the Lord, sent by Him to thee to tell thee that thy prayers have been heard, and that thy charitable deeds have gone up into His presence. For He hath seen thy shame, and hath heard the reproach of unfruitfulness which has been unjustly brought against thee. For God is the avenger of sin, not of nature: and, therefore, when He shuts up the womb of any one, He does so that He may miraculously open it again; so that that which is born may be acknowledged to be not of lust, but of the gift of God. For was it not the case that the first mother of your nation--Sarah--was barren up to her eightieth year? And, nevertheless, in extreme old age she brought forth Isaac, to whom the promise was renewed of the blessing of all nations. Rachel also, so favored of the Lord, and so beloved by holy Jacob, was long barren; and yet she brought forth Joseph, who was not only the lord of Egypt, but the deliverer of many nations who were ready to perish of hunger. Who among the judges was either stronger than Samson, or more holy than Samuel? And yet the mothers of both were barren. If, therefore, the reasonableness of my words does not persuade thee, believe in fact that conceptions very late in life, and births in the case of women that have been barren, are usually attended with something wonderful. Accordingly thy wife Anna will bring forth a daughter to thee, and thou shalt call her name Mary: she shall be, as you have vowed, consecrated to the Lord from her infancy, and she shall be filled with the Holy Spirit, even from her mother's womb. She shall neither eat nor drink any unclean thing, nor shall she spend her life among the crowds of the people without, but in the temple of the Lord, that it may not be possible either to say, or so much as to suspect, any evil concerning her. Therefore, when she has grown up, just as she herself shall be miraculously born of a barren woman, so in an incomparable manner she, a virgin, shall bring forth the Son of the Most High, who shall be called Jesus, and who, according to the etymology of His name, shall be the Savior of all nations. And this shall be the sign to thee of those things which I announce: When thou shalt come to the Golden gate in Jerusalem, thou shalt there meet Anna thy wife, who, lately anxious from the delay of thy return, will then rejoice at the sight of thee. Having thus spoken, the angel departed from him.

CHAPTER IV

Thereafter he appeared to Anna his wife, saying: Fear not, Anna, nor think that it is a phantom which thou seest. For I am that angel who has presented your prayers and alms before God; and now have I been sent to you to announce to you that thou shalt bring forth a daughter, who shall be called Mary, and who shall be blessed above all women. She, full of the favor of the Lord even from her birth, shall remain three years in her father's house until she be weaned. Thereafter, being delivered to the service of the Lord, she shall not depart from the temple until she reach the years of discretion. There, in fine, serving God day and night in fastings and prayers, she shall abstain from every unclean thing; she shall never know man, but alone, without example, immaculate, uncorrupted, without intercourse with man, she, a virgin, shall bring forth a son; she, His hand-maiden, shall bring forth the Lord--both in grace, and in name, and in work, the Savior of the world. Wherefore arise, and go up to Jerusalem; and when thou shalt come to the gate which, because it is plated with gold, is called Golden, there, for a sign, thou shalt meet thy husband, for whose safety thou hast been anxious. And when these things shall have so happened, know that what I announce shall without doubt be fulfilled.

CHAPTER V

Therefore, as the angel had commanded, both of them setting out from the place where they were, went up to Jerusalem; and when they had come to the place pointed out by the angel's prophecy, there they met each other. Then, rejoicing at seeing each other, and secure in the certainty of the promised offspring, they gave the thanks due to the Lord, who exalteth the humble. And so, having worshipped the Lord, they returned home, and awaited in certainty and in gladness the divine promise. Anna therefore conceived, and brought forth a daughter; and according to the command of the angel, her parents called her name Mary.

CHAPTER VI

And when the circle of three years had rolled round, and the time of her weaning was fulfilled, they brought the virgin to the temple of the Lord with offerings. Now there were round the temple, according to the fifteen Psalms of Degrees, fifteen steps going up; for, on account of the temple having been built on a mountain, the altar of burnt-offering, which stood outside, could not be reached except by steps. On one of these, then, her parents placed the little girl, the blessed virgin Mary. And when they were putting off the clothes which they had worn on the journey, and were putting on, as was usual, others that were neater and cleaner, the virgin of the Lord went up all the steps, one after the other, without the help of any one leading her or lifting her, in such a manner that, in this respect at least, you would think that she had already attained full age. For already the Lord in the infancy of His virgin wrought a great thing, and by the indication of this miracle foreshowed how great she was to be. Therefore, a sacrifice having been offered according to the custom of the law, and their vow being perfected, they left the virgin within the enclosures of the temple, there to be educated with the other virgins, and themselves returned home.

CHAPTER VII

But the virgin of the Lord advanced in age and in virtues; and though, in the words of the Psalmist, her father and mother had forsaken her, the Lord took her up. For daily was she visited by angels, daily did she enjoy a divine vision, which preserved her from all evil, and made her to abound in all good. And so she reached her fourteenth year; and not only were the wicked unable to charge her with anything worthy of reproach, but all the good, who knew her life and conversation, judged her to be worthy of admiration. Then the high priest publicly announced that the virgins who were publicly settled in the temple, and had reached this time of life, should return home and get married, according to the custom of the nation and the ripeness of their years. The others readily obeyed this command; but Mary alone, the virgin of the Lord, answered that she could not do this, saying both that her parents had devoted her to the service of the Lord, and that, moreover, she herself had made to the Lord a vow of virginity, which she would never violate by any intercourse with man. And the high priest, being placed in great perplexity of mind, seeing that neither did he think that the vow should be broken contrary to the Scripture, which says, Vow and pay, nor did he dare to introduce a custom unknown to the nation, gave order that at the festival, which was at hand, all the chief persons from Jerusalem and the neighborhood should be present, in order that from their advice he might know what was to be done in so doubtful a case. And when this took place, they resolved unanimously that the Lord should be consulted upon this matter. And when they all bowed themselves in prayer, the high priest went to consult God in the usual way. Nor had they long to wait: in the hearing of all a voice issued from the oracle and from the mercy-seat, that, according to the prophecy of Isaiah, a man should be sought out to whom the virgin ought to be entrusted and espoused. For it is clear that Isaiah says: A rod shall come forth from the root of Jesse, and a flower shall ascend from his root; and the Spirit of the Lord shall rest upon him, the spirit of wisdom and understanding, the spirit of counsel and strength, the spirit of wisdom and piety; and he shall be filled with the spirit of the fear of the Lord. According to this prophecy, therefore, he predicted that all of the house and family of David that were unmarried and fit for marriage should bring there rods to the altar; and that he whose rod after it was brought should produce a flower, and upon the end of whose rod the Spirit of the Lord should settle in the form of a dove, was the man to whom the virgin ought to be entrusted and espoused.

CHAPTER VIII

Now there was among the rest Joseph, of the house and family of David, a man of great age: and when all brought there rods, according to the order, he alone withheld his. Wherefore, when nothing in conformity with the divine voice appeared, the high priest thought it necessary to consult God a second time; and He answered, that of those who had been designated, he alone to whom the virgin ought to be espoused had not brought his rod. Joseph, therefore, was found out. For when he had brought his rod, and the dove came from heaven; and settled upon the top of it, it clearly appeared to all that he was the man to whom the virgin should be espoused. Therefore, the usual ceremonies of betrothal having been gone through, he went back to the city of Bethlehem to put his house in order, and to procure things necessary for the marriage. But Mary, the virgin of the Lord, with seven other virgins of her own age, and who had been weaned at the same time, whom she had received from the priest, returned to the house of her parents in Galilee.

CHAPTER IX

And in those days, that is, at the time of her first coming into Galilee, the angel Gabriel was sent to her by God, to announce to her the conception of the Lord, and to explain to her the manner and order of the conception. Accordingly, going in, he filled the chamber where she was with a great light; and most courteously saluting her, he said: Hail, Mary! O virgin highly favored by the Lord, virgin full of grace, the Lord is with thee; blessed art thou above all women, blessed above all men that have been hitherto born. And the virgin, who was already well acquainted with angelic faces, and was not unused to the light from heaven, was neither terrified by the vision of the angel, nor astonished at the greatness of the light, but only perplexed by his words; and she began to consider of what nature a salutation so unusual could be, or what it could portend, or what end it could have. And the angel, divinely inspired, taking up this thought, says: Fear not, Mary, as if anything contrary to thy chastity were hid under this salutation. For in choosing chastity, thou hast found favor with the Lord; and therefore thou, a virgin, shalt conceive without sin, and shalt bring forth a son. He shall be great, because He shall rule from sea to sea, and from the river even to the ends of the earth; and He shall be called the Son of the Most High, because He who is born on earth in humiliation, reigns in heaven in exaltation; and the Lord God will give Him the throne of His father David, and He shall reign in the house of Jacob for ever, and of His kingdom there shall be no end; forasmuch as He is King of kings and Lord of lords, and His throne is from everlasting to everlasting. The virgin did not doubt these words of the angel; but wishing to know the manner of it, she answered: How can that come to pass? For while, according to my vow, I never know man, how can I bring forth without the addition of man's seed? To this the angel says: Think not, Mary, that thou shalt conceive in the manner of mankind: for without any intercourse with man, thou, a virgin, wilt conceive; thou, a virgin, wilt bring forth; thou, a virgin, wilt nurse: for the Holy Spirit shall come upon thee, and the power of the Most High shall overshadow thee, without any of the heats of lust; and therefore that which shall be born of thee shall alone be holy, because it alone, being conceived and born without sin, shall be called the Son of God. Then Mary stretched forth her hands, and raised her eyes to heaven, and said: Behold the handmaiden of the Lord, for I am not worthy of the name of lady; let it be to me according to thy word.

It will be long, and perhaps to some even tedious, if we insert in this little work everything which we read of as having preceded or followed the Lord's nativity: wherefore, omitting those things which have been more fully written in the Gospel, let us come to those which are held to be less worthy of being narrated.

CHAPTER X

Joseph therefore came from Judaea into Galilee, intending to marry the virgin who had been betrothed to him; for already three months had elapsed, and it was the beginning of the fourth since she had been betrothed to him. In the meantime, it was evident from her shape that she was pregnant, nor could she conceal this from Joseph. For in consequence of his being betrothed to her, coming to her more freely and speaking to her more familiarly, he found out that she was with child. He began then to be in great doubt and perplexity, because he did not know what was best for him to do. For, being a just man, he was not willing to expose her; nor, being a pious man, to injure her fair fame by a suspicion of fornication. He came to the conclusion, therefore, privately to dissolve their contract, and to send her away secretly. And while he thought on these things, behold, an angel of the Lord appeared to him in his sleep, saying: Joseph, thou son of David, fear not; that is, do not have any suspicion of fornication in the virgin, or think any evil of her; and fear not to take her as thy wife: for that which is begotten in her, and which now vexes thy soul, is the work not of man, but of the Holy Spirit. For she alone of all virgins shall bring forth the Son of God, and thou shalt call His name Jesus, that is, Savior; for He shall save His people from their sins. Therefore Joseph, according to the command of the angel, took the virgin as his wife; nevertheless he knew her not, but took care of her, and kept her in chastity. And now the ninth month from her conception was at hand, when Joseph, taking with him his wife along with what things he needed, went to

Bethlehem, the city from which he came. And it came to pass, while they were there, that her days were fulfilled that she should bring forth; and she brought forth her first-born son, as the holy evangelists have shown, our Lord Jesus Christ, who with the Father and the Son and the Holy Ghost lives and reigns God from everlasting to everlasting.

www.ingramcontent.com/pod-product-compliance
Lightning Source LLC
LaVergne TN
LVHW041500070426
835507LV00009B/721